THE LIBRARY (KTW)
Kent and Sussex Hospital
Postgraduate Medical Centre
Mount Ephraim, Tunbridge Wells
Kent TN4 8AT
01892 526111 ext 2384
fax 01892 531975

Books must be returned/renewed by the last date shown

Preface

This third book in the **Day-2-Day** series focuses on the major urological cancers. I am sure everyone will agree that this is a constantly evolving field of urology, and cannot be summarised fully in such a book.

However, the aim again is not to provide a replacement for the standard urology textbooks. Rather, the essential features of each condition and its management are summarised. I hope this overview of urological cancers will be of use in your day-2-day practice.

Jyoti Shah

Acknowledgements

I would like to express my sincere thanks to Alan. His assistance and knowledge have been invaluable. I would also like to thank Nim for his encouragement, and Rod and Jane of Eurocommunica for publishing this third book in the **Day-2-Day** series.

Finally, I would like to thank Abbott for providing financial assistance.

Foreword

It occurs to me that there are too many books on postgraduate medicine. They are big, written by many hands, slow to produce and expensive.

The problem is particularly great in Urology, because rapid advances make the classic text outdated almost as soon as the ink is dry. Consultants of my generation are performing few, if any, of the operations learnt as a registrar.

Therefore, I am delighted to introduce this book, which represents a clean break with tradition. In it, Jyoti Shah covers a subject in which there have been major developments in the last few years. It has been produced rapidly and yet provides a comprehensive review with economy of text.

In spite of the size, the critical pieces of information for daily management of patients are included. When it becomes outdated, it may be thrown away with a clear conscience but, by then, a new edition will be available!

CRJ Woodhouse
Consultant Urologist
The Royal Marsden Hospital
London

Contents

Abbreviations

ACT	alpha-antichymotrypsin
BCG	*Bacillus calmette-guérin*
bcl-2	human proto-oncogene located on chromosome 18
BPH	benign prostatic hyperplasia
CC	chemical cystitis
C-erbB	human proto-oncogene
ChT	chemotherapy
CIS	carcinoma in situ
CT	computed tomography
CXR	chest X-ray
Da	Daltons
DHT	dihydrotestosterone
DRE	digital rectal examination
DXT	radiotherapy
FSH	follicle stimulating hormone
GM-CSF	granulocyte-macrophage colony stimulating factor
HIV	human immunodeficiency virus
IAS	intermittent androgen suppression
ICSC	intermittent clean self catheterisation
ICSI	intracytoplasmic sperm injection
IGF-1	insulin-like growth factor
IVC	inferior vena cava
IVP	intravenous pyelogram
LH	luteinising hormone
LHRH	luteinising hormone-releasing hormone
MAB	maximum androgen blockade
MRI	magnetic resonance imaging
Nd-YAG	neodyium-yttrium aluminium garnet
PA	posteroanterior
PDGF	platelet-derived growth factor
PIN	prostatic intraepithelial neoplasia
PSA	prostate-specific antigen
PSAD	prostate-specific antigen density

RB	retinoblastoma
RCC	renal cell carcinoma
RP	radical prostatectomy
RR	recurrence rate
RSS	renal sparing surgery
SCCs	squamous cell cancers
TB	tuberculosis
TCCs	transitional cell cancers
TURBT	transurethral resection of bladder tumour
TURP	transurethral resection of prostate
5-FU	5-fluorouracil

Definitions

Incidence rate of a cancer
- the number of new cases diagnosed per 100,000 persons/year

Prevalence of a cancer
- total number of cancer cases present per 100,000 persons

Mortality rate of a cancer
- number of deaths occurring per 100,000 persons/year

Renal Cancer

Synonymous terms: renal cell carcinoma; clear cell carcinoma; hypernephroma

Incidence:
- 3% of all adult cancers
- 85% of all primary renal tumours

Age:
- 4th–6th decades

Male : Female ratio:
- 2:1

Classical triad:
- pain, haematuria and flank mass
- present in <10% of patients

Presentation:
- 23% will have lymph node metastases
- 5–7% will have renal vein metastases
- multifocality of RCCs: 7–20%
- main renal vein invasion: 21–35%

Common site of metastases:
- lung (75%)
- soft tissues (36%)
- bone (20%)
- liver (18%)
- cutaneous (8%)
- brain (8%)

Origin:
- commonly proximal convoluted tubular epithelium

Risk factors:
- smoking
  - at least 2-fold increase in risk
  - only consistent risk factor
  - cigarettes, pipes and cigars

- cystic changes in kidney – dialysis patients are at 30-fold increased risk
- obesity, especially in women
- hypertension
- unopposed oestrogen therapy
- occupational exposure to petroleum products/asbestos/tanning products

Forms: *Inherited*

1. Autosomal dominant
   - bilateral and multifocal
   - usually structural changes of chromosome 3
2. Von Hippel Lindau disease
3. Hereditary papillary renal carcinoma

Sporadic

GENETICS OF RENAL CANCER

- overexpression of c-myc, c-Ha-ras, c-fos, c-fms, f-raf-1 and c-erbB-1
- underexpression of HER-2 mRNA

HISTOLOGICAL TYPES

1. Clear cell carcinoma (75–85%)
2. Chromophilic (papillary) (14%)
3. Chromophobic (4%)
4. Oncocytic (2%)
5. Collecting duct (Bellini's duct) (<1%)

ROBSON STAGING

I	tumour confined within kidney parenchyma (no involvement of perinephric fat, renal vein or regional lymph node)
II	tumour involves perinephric fat, but is confined within Gerota's fascia (including adrenal)
IIIA	tumour involves main renal vein or IVC
IIIB	tumour involves regional lymph nodes
IIIC	tumour involves both local vessels and regional lymph nodes
IVA	tumour involves adjacent organs other than adrenal (colon, pancreas, etc)
IVB	distant metastases

TNM CLASSIFICATION (1997)
T – Primary Tumour

TX	● tumour cannot be assessed
T0	● no evidence of primary tumour
T1	● tumour ≤7cm limited to kidney
T2	● tumour >7cm limited to kidney
T3	● tumour extends into major veins or invades adrenal gland or perinephric tissues, but not beyond Gerota's fascia
T3a	● tumour invades adrenal gland or perinephric tissues, but not beyond Gerota's fascia
T3b	● tumour grossly extends into renal vein(s) or vena cava, below diaphragm
T3c	● tumour grossly extends into vena cava above diaphragm
T4	● tumour invades beyond Gerota's fascia

N – Regional Lymph Nodes

NX	● regional lymph nodes cannot be assessed
N0	● no regional lymph node metastases
N1	● lymph node metastases in a single regional lymph node
N2	● metastases in more than a single regional lymph node

M – Distant Metastases

MX   ● distant metastases cannot be assessed
M0   ● no distant metastases
M1   ● distant metastases present

COMPARISON OF ROBSON AND TNM CLASSIFICATIONS

Robson	TNM	Comment
I	T1	Small tumour (confined to renal capsule)
I	T2	Large tumour/calyceal distortion (confined to renal capsule)
II	T3a	Tumour extension to perineal fat or ipsilateral adrenal gland (within Gerota's fascia)
IIIa	T3b	Renal vein involved
IIIa	T3c	Renal vein and IVC involved
IIIa	T4b	IVC involved above diaphragm
IIIb	N1	Single ipsilateral node involved
IIIb	N2	Multiple regional/contralateral or bilateral nodes involved
IIIc	T3, 4 N1, 2	Combination of IIIa and IIIb
IVa	T4a	Spread to contiguous organs, except ipsilateral adrenal gland
IVb	M1	Distant metastases

FUHRMAN SYSTEM FOR NUCLEAR GRADE

Grade	Nuclear Grade
I	Small (10mm), round, uniform nuclei with inconspicuous or absent nuclei
II	Medium-sized (15mm) nuclei with irregularities in outline and small nucleoli
III	Large (20mm) nuclei with obviously irregular outline and prominent nucleoli
IV	Grade 3 nuclei with addition of bizarre, often multilobulated nuclei possessing heavy chromatin clumps

IMAGING STUDIES

1. CT Scan
Percentage of time correct diagnosis made

Case	Percentage
Renal vein involvement	91%
IVC extension	97%
Perirenal extension	79%
Lymph node metastases	87%
Extension to adjacent organs	96%

2. MRI Scan
- less accurate then CT scan for lesions <2–3cm
- 94% sensitivity for renal vein involvement

- 100% sensitivity for IVC involvement
- 80% sensitivity for right atrial involvement

3. Bone Scan
- 93% sensitivity for metastases
- 86% specificity for metastases

PROGNOSIS
1. Factors associated with local regional disease

Factor	Comment	5-year survival
Stage of tumour (most important)	Robson Stage I	75%
	Stage II	63%
	Stage III	38%
	Stage IV	11%
Size of tumour	Better when <5cm; poor >10cm	
Cell type	Worse when spindle cell	
Nuclear grade		
Histological type	Poor if renal adenocarcinoma and sarcomatoid component	
Renal vein involvement		
Extension to regional nodes		0–30%
Extension through Gerota's fascia		45%
Involvement of contiguous organs		<5%
Distant metastases		-

2. Factors associated with metastatic disease
- long disease-free interval between nephrectomy and metastasis
- excellent performance status
- pulmonary metastasis only
- no weight loss
- no prior chemotherapy

TREATMENT FOR LOCALISED RENAL CARCINOMA
1. Radical nephrectomy
- excision of adrenal gland, perinephric fat and hilar lymphatics
- value of routine lymphadenectomy questionable
- occasional benefit to preoperative angiographic renal vein occlusion for large tumours

Approaches to kidney
Open:
- flank
- thoracoabdominal
- anterior

Laparoscopic:
- transperitoneal
- retroperitoneal

Five-year survival after radical nephrectomy

Stage	5-year survival
Stage I	60–82%
Stage II	47–80%
Stage III	35–51%
Stage IV	Almost 0% (median survival 20 months)

2. Partial nephrectomy
- ideal for small tumours
- 100% 5-year survival rate for <4cm incidental RCCs
- local recurrence rate 6–10%

3. Renal-sparing surgery (RSS)
- ideal for solitary kidney or bilaterally occurring tumours
- techniques include enucleation, wedge resection, polar amputation

Survival data for RSS

Surgical indication	Survival comment
Tumour in solitary kidney	5-year survival 70–85%
Bilateral tumours	5-year survival 50–75%
Complete tumour removal (single/bilateral)	3-year disease-free survival 72%
Risk of local tumour recurrence	2–10%

4. The role of radiotherapy (DXT)
Pre-operative:

Stage	2-year survival		5-year survival	
	Neph + DXT	Nephrectomy (Neph) alone	Neph + DXT	Nephrectomy (Neph) alone
Stage I	90%	90%	85%	88%
Stage II	68%	52%	62%	64%
Stage III	–	–	27%	29%

Post-operative:
- can usually start 3–6 weeks after nephrectomy

Indications:
- residual tumour in renal fossa
- tumour transected during surgery
- tumour spillage during surgery
- T3a, T3b, T4, N1, N2

Stage	Treatment modality	5-year survival	Recurrence rate
T1-T4	Nephrectomy alone Nephrectomy + post-op DXT	52% 25%	- -
T2-T4	Nephrectomy alone Nephrectomy + post-op DXT	40% 50%	19% 9%
All stages	Nephrectomy alone Nephrectomy + post-op DXT	18–47% 36–38%	15–25% 7–13%
Stage II/III	Nephrectomy alone Nephrectomy + post-op DXT	63% 50%	3% 0%

Conclusions:
- unclear evidence
- no established role for routine pre- or post-operative radiotherapy

METASTATIC RENAL CELL CARCINOMA
IVC involvement
- 13% incidence with right-sided tumours
- 4.5% incidence with left-sided tumours
- 50% of the above are likely to have distant metastases

- 1–3% with metastases will have a solitary lesion
  - 35% 5-year survival with solitary lesion
  - median survival 4.3 years
- 0.8% lesions spontaneously regress
- 5-year survival after complete excision of IVC tumour thrombus is 47–69%
- Larger thrombi that require cardiopulmonary bypass have 3-year survival rate of 64%

1. Palliative Nephrectomy

- to control symptoms
- median survival of 4 months
- 10% 1-year survival rate

2. Palliative Radiotherapy
Indications:

- pain relief successful to death in 65–83% patients
- prevent impending fracture
- spinal cord compression
- metastatic brain disease

3. Chemotherapy

- RCCs are amongst the most chemoresistant tumours
- responses to cytotoxic chemotherapy rarely exceeds 10% for any regimen that has been studied with adequate numbers

4. Biological Response Modifiers

a. Alpha-Interferon
(α-IFN)
- 11–15% treatment response in clinical trials
- 2% complete response
- response appears to be in patients who have non-bulky pulmonary or soft tissue metastases
- promising future

b. Interleukin-2 (IL-2)
- complete response in 4–5%
- overall response in 10–15% patients
- median duration of response of 23.2 months
- <2% treatment-related mortality

c. Combination of IL-2 and α-IFN
- many studies have failed to show that this potent combination is better than IL-2 alone
- response is increased if above combination is used with fluorouracil (47% response rate; 11% complete responses)

Bladder Cancer

Synonymous terms: urothelial cancer

Incidence:
- most common site of cancer in the urinary tract
- 90% of all bladder cancers are transitional cell cancers (TCCs) (varies with geography)

Median age of presentation:
- 69–70 years

Male : Female ratio:
- 2.5:1 (UK)

Country	New cases per year	Sex	% of all new cancer cases	% of cancer deaths
UK	12,900	Male	7.9	4.4
		Female	3.2	2.4
USA	50,000	Male	6.3	2.9
		Female	2.5	1.5

Aetiology:
- age

Age group	Incidence in each age category	
	Male	Female
65–69 years	130	35
Over 85 years	285	65

- cigarette smoking
    - 50% of all cases in men
    - 31% of cases in women
- occupational exposure: benzidine, β-napthylamine, 4-aminobiphenyl
- chronic infection
- schistosomiasis (squamous cell more common)
- pelvic radiotherapy
- heavy analgesic use, especially phenacetin
- cytotoxic agents, such as cyclophosphamide
- instrumentation, calculi, trauma to urothelium, indwelling catheter – all risk factors for squamous cancers

GENETICS OF BLADDER CANCER
Multi-stage carcinogenesis:

- Deletions of chromosome 9p – most common in superficial cancers
- Deletions of chromosome 17q – 60% of invasive cancers
- Deletions of chromosome 11p, leading to overexpression of c-Ha-ras oncogene and its product p21 – 40% of invasive bladder cancers (ras and p21 pathways are key molecular pathways that promote G1-S transition in cell cycle)

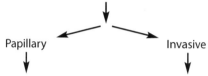

- p53 mutations (loss of normal or wild-type p53 expression leads to loss of apoptosis or programmed cell death)

Papillary   Invasive

10-15% progress to higher stage disease

80% have no previous history of superficial disease

PATHOLOGY

1. Transitional cell cancers
2. Adenocarcinomas
3. Squamous cancers
4. Sarcomas
5. Mixed cancers

- 90% of all bladder cancers
- 2%
- 3–7%
- 2%
- 3–6%

PRESENTATION

>70% patients present with haematuria

Diagnostic approach: Tri-fold test approach increases sensitivity and specificity

1. Urine Cytology
   - more sensitive in high-grade tumours/CIS
   - approx 20% of these will have false-negatives
   - 1-12% false-positive cytology
   - ideally obtain first-voided morning specimen
   - artefactually altered by UTI,

> bladder instrumentation,
> indwelling catheters, DXT and
> intravesical immuno- or
> chemotherapy

2. IVU – low specificity if bladder tumour <0.5cm in diameter

3. Cystoscopy (flexible or rigid)

TNM CLASSIFICATION (1997)
T – Primary Tumour

TX	● primary tumour cannot be evaluated
T0	● no primary tumour
Ta	● non-invasive papillary carcinoma
Tis	● carcinoma *in situ*
T1	● tumour invades lamina propria under the epithelium
T1a	● superficial submucosal invasion
T1b	● deep submucosal invasion
T2	● tumour invades muscle
T2a	● superficial muscle affected
T2b	● deep muscle affected
T3	● tumour invades perivesical fatty tissue
T3a	● microscopic perivesical invasion
T3b	● macroscopic perivesical invasion
T4	● tumour invades any of the following: prostate, uterus, vagina, pelvic wall, abdominal wall
T4a	● tumour invades prostate, uterus or vagina

| T4b | ● tumour invades pelvic wall or abdominal wall |

N – Regional Lymph Nodes

NX	● regional lymph nodes cannot be evaluated
N0	● no regional lymph node metastasis
N1	● metastasis in a single lymph node ≤2cm in size
N2	● metastasis in a single lymph node >2cm and <5cm in size, or multiple lymph nodes <5cm in size
N3	● metastasis in a lymph node >5cm in size

M – Distant Metastases

MX	● distant metastasis cannot be evaluated
M0	● no distant metastasis
M1	● distant metastasis

Additional Descriptors may be Added to TNM:

Suffix	**Definition**
m	synchronous multiple tumours within bladder
is	associated carcinoma *in situ*
y	classification was made during or following other treatment, e.g. surgery
r	tumour is a recurrence in a previously treated area
R	residual tumour after treatment (R1=macro- and R2=microscopic)

C-factor category –
where evidence of tumour arises from:

C1	● standard diagnostic means, such as clinical presentation
C2	● special diagnostic means, such as CT or MRI imaging
C3	● surgical exploration
C4	● pathological examination of therapeutically resected specimen
C5	● autopsy evidence

GRADE

Grade I	well-differentiated tumour
Grade II	moderately differentiated tumour
Grade III	poorly differentiated tumour

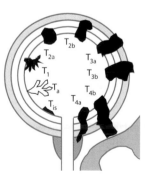

Staging

Probability of positive pelvic lymph node metastasis by tumour stage

Clinical stage	Positive pelvic nodes (%)
Tis	0
Ta	6
T1	10
T2	16
T3a	20
T3b, T4	25-33

Cancer-specific survival rates after radical cystectomy

Pathological factor		5-year survival (%)	10-year survival (%)
T-stage	Tis, Ta, T1	82	71
	T2	64	48
	T3, T4	39	23
Nodal Status	N-	67	50
	N+	21	17
Tumour grade	Grade 1	-	98
	Grade 2	-	87
	Grade 3	-	35

Behaviour of bladder cancer after 3 years

Stage	Recurrence	Progression
Ta	50%	<10%
T1	>70%	>30%
Grade	Recurrence	Progression
G1-2	50-60%	<10%
G3	80%	>50%

MANAGEMENT OF SUPERFICIAL BLADDER CANCERS
T classification of superficial bladder cancers – Ta, T1, Tis

Poor prognostic factors of superficial bladder tumours

Number of tumours at presentation	N >1
Recurrence at 1st check cystoscopy (R)	R = 1 – moderate risk R >1/year – high risk
T category	T1 worse than Ta
G grade	G3
Tumour diameter	>3cm
Tumour configuration	Sessile worse than papillary
Urine cytology	Positive (tends to correlate with G3/CIS)
Carcinoma *in situ*	Present = high risk

Predictors of progression of superficial tumours

	G1	G2	G3
Ta	8–9% in total		53% any stage
T1	4%	33%	

Significance of depth of invasion and grade on 5-year survival for superficial bladder cancer

Stage and Grade	5-year survival (%)
Ta, Grade 1, 2	98
T1, Grade 2	83
T1, Grade 3	63

Tumour-free time after initial resection of a superficial bladder tumour (any stage and grade)

Time after initial tumour	Chance of developing another recurrence
2 years	43%
5 years	22%

TREATMENT OPTIONS

1. Surgery
- transurethral resection of bladder tumours (TURBT)

2. Laser
- useful for tumours that are papillary and appear low grade
- can be used in patients with history of low-grade and low-stage tumours

3. Intravesical therapy
- 3 aims:
  a. to reduce risk of recurrence and therefore reduce frequency of cystoscopic follow-up (single treatment)
  b. to reduce number of recurrences in multifocal disease (course of treatment)
  c. to prevent progression to muscle-invasive disease (course of treatment)

Intravesical Agents

Name	Generic name	Type of agent	Molecular weight (DA)	Cell cycle-specific?	Adverse effects
Thiotepa	Triethylene-thiophos-phoramide	Alkylating agent	198	No	25% risk of leucopenia and thrombo-cytopenia due to systemic absorption; 12–69% risk of chemical cystitis (CC)
Doxorubicin (Adriamycin)	Produced by *Streptomyces peucetius*	Anthra-cycline antibiotic	580	No (max effect in S-phase)	20–30% risk of CC
Mitomycin C	Produced by *Streptomyces caespitosus*	Antibiotic	329	No (most active in S- and G-phases)	6–41% risk of CC
Epirubicin	4'-epidoxo-rubicin	Epimere of doxorubicin		No	As with doxorubicin

Response rates for intravesical agents in superficial bladder cancer

Name	Dose	Response rate when used as definitive treatment	Recurrence rate	Use as an adjuvant agent after TURBT	Use in treatment of CIS
Thiotepa	30mg	38%	45%	17% advantage over control	Less valuable
Doxorubicin	50mg	28–56%	38%	18%	34%
Mitomycin C	40–60mg	43%	37%	15% advantage to control	58%
Epirubicin	80mg	56%	–	–	–
BCG	Depends upon strain	50–60%	31%	44%	70%

a. Recurrent superficial disease

- time to first recurrence significantly prolonged by doxorubicin (recurrence rate [RR] per year was 0.30) compared with TURBT alone (RR = 0.68)

b. Progression to invasive disease by adjuvant treatments

- for stage Ta, T1 tumours ~20% decrease in risk of superficial recurrence in those with adjuvant chemotherapy versus TURBT alone
- no long-term benefit in progression to muscle-invasive disease demonstrated

c. Time of adjuvant treatment

- single early installation of 80mg epirubicin <6 hours after TURBT prolonged time to first recurrence (RR = 0.16) compared to TURBT alone (RR = 0.40)
- this study demonstrated a 12% reduction in tumour recurrence

4. Intravesical immunotherapy

- *Bacillus calmette-guérin* (BCG) = live attenuated TB vaccine
- first-line treatment for CIS and T1G3 tumours

Two requirements for BCG to work:

- needs to be in direct contact with tumour
- patient must have T-lymphocytes

Contraindications for BCG:

- immunocompromised patients (HIV-positive patients)
- patients on immunosuppressive treatments
- leukaemia
- Hodgkin's disease
- pregnant women
- lactating females

Adverse effects:

- 5% risk of serious adverse events with BCG, including systemic TB –

treat with 6 months of anti-TB drugs
- 3% patients have fevers (most common reaction)
- BCG cystitis (treat with isoniazid)
- arthralgia
- ureteric obstruction (treat with surgical reimplantation)

Three clinical uses of BCG:

a. Prophylaxis in superficial cancers
- comparison of TURBT alone with adjuvant BCG
- RR 75% for TURBT alone, but 31% with BCG
- 44% net benefit for BCG

b. Treatment of superficial cancers
- not a substitute for resectable tumours
- complete response rate of 58% – need to wait at least 2 weeks after TURBT (ideally 3-4 weeks) before starting BCG

c. Treatment of CIS
- first choice of treatment for this condition
- 30% of patients do not respond to BCG as first-line treatment
- 30% of initial responders will relapse at 5 years
- at 10 years, only 31% are tumour-free
- 53% of patients respond to a second course of BCG after failing the first course

CURRENT GUIDELINES FOR INTRAVESICAL TREATMENT OF SUPERFICIAL BLADDER TUMOURS

1. Low-risk patients
- primary, small, solitary and low-grade Ta tumours
- low risk of progression
- hence intravesical treatment not indicated

2. Low progression risk
- high risk of recurrence
- single dose of 80mg epirubicin <6 hours after TURBT
- single dose 40mg mitomycin-C immediately after TURBT

3. High progression risk
- high grade (G3) and/or high stage (T1) tumours/multifocal recurrence or patients with diffuse CIS
- TURBT with adjuvant intravesical treatment with BCG
- no consensus on length of BCG treatment

Current guidelines suggest:
- induction course of 6-weekly treatments
- cystoscopy and biopsy at 6 weeks after end of treatment

CIS settling:
- second induction course with up to 2 years' maintenance

**CIS not settling
+/- progression:**
- immediate cystectomy

FOLLOW-UP CYSTOSCOPIES
- first check at 3 months unless G3/CIS
- if pT1b disease, then first check at 6 weeks

Thereafter:
- according to clinical need
- low risk – annual check
- moderate risk – 6-monthly for 2 years, then annually
- high risk – 3-monthly until stable, then as for moderate risk

MANAGEMENT OF INVASIVE BLADDER CANCER
- untreated 3-year survival of 5%

1. Radical TURBT
- to stage tumours
- treat with view of offering normal bladder function and potency
- rationale based on fact that 10–15% of patients have pathological stage P0 at cystectomy following TURBT
- must adhere to strict surveillance schedule

Indications:
- small tumours with superficial

muscle invasion (T2)
- no evidence of CIS
- medically unfit for cystectomy

Five-year survival with TURBT alone

Study	Number of patients	5-year survival for T2 or T3a
Solsona E et al 1992	59	73%
Henry K et al 1988	43	52%
Herr HW 1987	45	68%
Barnes RW et al 1977	114	40%
O'Flynn JD et al 1975	123	52%
Flocks RH 1951	142	47%

2. Partial cystectomy
- allows normal bladder function and potency
- less morbidity than cystectomy

Indications:
- solitary tumour
- no CIS
- excision allows 2cm tumour-free margin
- no bladder neck, base or prostatic involvement
- no history of previous or non-bladder urothelial malignancy

Outcome:
- 5-year survival rate for T2 tumours is 30–60%

- high rate of local recurrence, 38–78% – may still need radical cystectomy

3. Radical cystectomy

Men
- removal of bladder, prostate, seminal vesicles, perivesical fat, pelvic peritoneum, urachal remnant

Women
- removal of bladder, urethra, anterior vaginal wall, ovaries, fallopian tubes, uterus, pelvic peritoneum, urachal remnant

Five-year survival data for radical cystectomy

Stage	5-year survival
pT2	63–88%
pT3a	50–69%
Invasive organ-confined disease (pT2 or pT3a)	64–83%
pT3b	15–46%
pT4	18–29%
N1 or N2 disease	Approx 30%

Urethrectomy
- most important with prostatic urethral involvement
- tumour recurrence in its absence is <15%

● with prostate involvement,
  recurrence rate is 37%

4. Radiotherapy (DXT) alone

● there are no controlled trials
  comparing surgery + DXT; DXT
  patients tend to have more
  extensive disease and are less fit –
  thus difficult to directly compare
  the two treatment modalities

Treatment Modality	Mean 5-year survival
Cystectomy alone	79%
High-dose external beam DXT	36%

Study	No. of patients	Stage	5-year survival	10-year survival	Local tumour control rate
Duncan and Quilty 1986	963	T1-T4	36%	18%	24%
Goodman GB et al 1981	470	B (77%) C (23%)	32%	22%	58%

Conclusion: ● 18-20% of T2-T4 patients may
              experience cure with primary
              DXT alone

Age-specific Survival

Study	Stage	Age group	5-year survival
Fossa SD *et al* 1993	T2 or T3a	≤ 75 years	46%
		> 75 years	20%

Stage	5-year survival data
T1	35%
T2	40%
T3a	35%
T3b and T4	20%
N1, N2	7%

5. Primary DXT + Salvage Cystectomy
Aims:
- treat microscopic local disease extension and nodal micrometastatic disease
- downstaging primary tumour
- ease of operability of lesion
- increase local disease control

Only 8–15% of patients eligible for cystectomy (advanced age, health, metastatic disease)

- this restricts overall impact of strategy on survival

Results of primary DXT plus salvage cystectomy for bladder cancer

Study	5-year survival	Complication (mortality)
Yu WS et al 1985	51%	30% (NR)
Goffinet DR et al 1975	48%	-
Smith and Whitmore 1981	32%	29% (5%)
Crawford and Skinner 1980	<38%	28% (8%)

(NR – not reported)

Conclusion: ● little benefit for pre-operative DXT for muscle-invasive disease

6. Pre-operative DXT + Cystectomy (DXT + Cy) versus DXT (DXT) alone

Stage	No. of patients	5-year survival	
		DXT + Cy	DXT alone
T3	199 patients		
		38%	29%
	Patients <60 years	41%	25%
Stage B2	68 patients	46%	16%

Conclusion: ● two randomised trials suggest that the use of cystectomy improves local control and survival compared to DXT alone

7. Pre-operative DXT + Cystectomy (DXT + Cy) versus Cystectomy (Cy) alone

Stage	No. of patients	5-year survival		Statistically significant?
		DXT + Cy	Cy alone	
T2-T4 tumours	234 patients	45%	35%	No
		8-year survival 19% for both modalities		
	148 patients	40%	51%	No
T2 or T3a G3	51 patients	77%	68%	No

Conclusion: ● 3 prospective randomised trials show no benefit for routine pre-operative DXT

8. Post-operative DXT
78 patients had combined pre-operative and post-operative DXT

Stage	Overall survival
pT2	57%
pT3a	58%
pT3b	39%
pT4/N+	50%

Incidence of bowel obstruction:
● 37% with post-operative DXT
● 8% without post-operative DXT

Conclusion:
● unacceptably high morbidity
● no demonstrable advantage of post-operative DXT

9. Initial Chemotherapy followed by DXT (ChT + DXT)

Stage	ChT	No. of patients	Survival		
			Follow-up	DXT alone	ChT + DXT
T2-T4	Cisplatin	255 patients	3 years	40%	40%
T2-T4	Multi-agent	47 patients	3 years		73%
T2-T4	Multi-agent	29 patients	4.75 years		71%

Conclusion: ● although cisplatin appears to be of benefit, two small trials of multi-agent chemotherapy show promise

10. Initial DXT followed by Chemotherapy (DXT + ChT)

Stage	Follow-up period	No. of patients	Survival	
			DXT alone	ChT + DXT
T3	5 years	129 patients	30%	30%
T3	3 years	376 patients	34%	39%

Conclusion: ● based on the data, there appears to be no use for adjuvant ChT when used with DXT

11. Concomitant ChT + DXT

Stage	No. of patients	ChT	Follow-up time	Survival
T2-T4	48 patients	Cisplatin	3 years	64%
T1-T4	139 patients	Cisplatin	5.9 years	52%
T2-T4	99 patients	Cisplatin + DXT	2 years	61%
		DXT alone		30%
T2-T4	20 patients	5-FU	5 years	40%
T3-T4	36 patients	5-FU + DXT	3 years	17%
		DXT alone		17%

Conclusion:

- concomitant ChT is better than DXT alone for early response and survival rates. In this sense, cisplatin is superior to 5-FU, based on increased toxicity with 5-FU

12. Single agent Systemic ChT

- variety of agents available with activity demonstrated in urothelial cancers

Single agent chemotherapy	Response rate (complete and partial)
5-fluorouracil (5-FU)	17%
Doxorubicin	17–19%
Carboplatin	13%
Cisplatin	24%
Cyclophosphamide	31%
Methotrexate	29%
Mitomycin C	13%
Vinblastine	16%

13. Combination Systemic ChT

Used:
- patients with unresectable cancers
- patients with metastatic cancers

Combinations used:

M-VAC
- methotrexate, vinblastine, doxorubicin, cisplatin

CMV
- cisplatin, methotrexate, vinblastine

CM
- cisplatin, methotrexate

CISCA /CAP
- cyclophosphamide, doxorubicin, cisplatin

Chemotherapy combination	No. of patients	Complete response rate
CM	293	14%
CMV	157	22%
CISCA	293	22%
M-VAC	526	20%

Combinations used	No. of patients	Response	Survival
CM vs cisplatin alone	108 patients	NS	NS
Cisplatin + cyclophosphamide vs cisplatin alone	109 patients	NS	NS
Cisplatin + doxorubicin (C+D) vs doxorubicin alone	78 patients	C + D	NS
M-VAC vs cisplatin	246 patients	M-VAC	M-VAC
M-VAC vs CISCA	110 patients	M-VAC	M-VAC

(NS = no significant difference)

Conclusion:
- M-VAC is superior to single agent therapy + CISCA
- M-VAC provides the most active regime

14. Neoadjuvant ChT

Stage	Treatment modality	Outcome	Follow-up
T3b, T4, N1-3	Cystectomy alone	54% survival	5 years
	Cystectomy + post-operative cisplatin	57% survival	
	Cystectomy alone	46% survival	3 years
	Cystectomy + CISCA	70% survival	
pT3b, PT4, N1	Cystectomy alone	13% progression-free survival	
	Cystectomy + M-VAC	58% progression-free survival	

Conclusion:
- combination chemotherapy results in long-term survival in 15-20% of patients only
- uncertain data regarding neoadjuvant chemotherapy prior to cystectomy
- adjuvant chemotherapy benefits pT3b, pN+ and pT4 disease

FUTURE DIRECTIONS
- aggressive treatment with cisplatin, 5-FU, high dose DXT in conjunction with selective bladder preservation
- tried in patients with T2-T4a, NX, M0
- 67% complete response rate and 66% 3-year survival rate

Renal Pelvis and Ureter Tumours

Incidence:
- 4–5% of all urothelial malignancies
- peak incidence in 7th decade
- bladder : renal pelvis : ureter ratio 51 : 3 : 1

Aetiology:
- cigarette smoking
- abuse of phenacetin-containing analgesics
- Balkan's nephropathy

Presentation:
- 60–80% of patients have haematuria
- 20–30% of patients have flank or abdominal pain
- 20–50% of patients have irritative symptoms (dysuria or frequency)

Pathology:
- 90% of renal pelvis tumours are TCCs
- 97% of ureteric tumours are TCCs
- 5-10% of tumours are SCCs

Risk of other tumours:
- 65–70% of ureteric tumours occur in distal 1/3 of ureter
- 50% multicentricity of ureteric cancer
- 1% risk of bilateral upper tract TCC

- 2–4% risk of contralateral upper tract TCC
- 30–50% risk of developing bladder cancer when have upper tract tumour
- <2% of bladder cancer patients have upper tract TCC

Diagnostic approach:
1. IVP
2. Cystoscopy and retrograde pyelogram
3. Ureteroscopy
4. CT scan

TNM CLASSIFICATION (1997)
T – Primary Tumour

TX	● tumour cannot be assessed
T0	● no evidence of primary tumour
Ta	● non-invasive papillary tumour
TIS	● carcinoma *in situ*
T1	● tumour invades subepithelial connective tissue
T2	● tumour invades the muscularis
T3	● (renal pelvis): tumour invades beyond muscularis into peripelvic fat or renal parenchyma
	● (ureter): tumour invades beyond muscularis into periureteric fat

T4   ● tumour invades adjacent organs or through kidney into perinephric fat

N – Regional Lymph Nodes

NX   ● nodes cannot be assessed
N0   ● no regional lymph node metastases
N1   ● metastasis in a single lymph node, ≤2cm in greatest dimension
N2   ● metastasis in a single lymph node, size 2–5cm; or multiple lymph nodes, none greater than 5cm in greatest dimension
N3   ● metastasis in a lymph node >5cm in greatest dimension

M – Distant Metastases

MX   ● distant metastasis cannot be assessed
M0   ● no distant metastasis
M1   ● distant metastases present

Overall 5-year Survival

Stage	5-year survival
T1 lesion or lower	90-100%
T2 lesion	40-80%
T3 lesion	15-30%
Metastatic carcinoma	5%

Grade	5-year survival	
	Renal pelvis tumour	Ureteric tumour
Well differentiated	100%	100%
Moderately well differentiated	90%	80%
Poorly differentiated	20-23%	28-30%

MANAGEMENT
1. Radical nephroureterectomy with excision of cuff of bladder

Rationale:
- multifocality of urothelial tumours
- high rate of local recurrence after incomplete tumour resection
- low incidence of contralateral renal involvement after radical nephroureterectomy

2. Non-invasive ureteric tumours can be treated conservatively in the following patient groups:
- functionally abnormal kidneys
- anatomically abnormal kidneys
- solitary kidney
- bilateral disease

Options:
- distal ureteric resection and reimplantation (psoas hitch/Boari flap)
- segmental resection of upper/mid ureter

3. Endourologic management

- ureteroscopic resection +/- fulguration

4. Intrapelvic/Intraureteric topical management

- thiopeta/mitomycin C/BCG
- few long-term reports available
- difficult to assess efficacy due to bias of patient population who undergo this form of treatment (poor surgical candidates, renal failure of single kidney)

SURVEILLANCE

- urine cytology, cystoscopy and upper tract imaging
- based on stage and grade of initial lesion

Prostate Cancer

Incidence:
- most common male malignancy in USA
- accounted for 30,000 deaths in 1999
- latent cancer found in up to 22% of post-mortem specimens

Age:
- 95% of cancers are detected in men 45–89 years (median age 72 years)

Geography:
- unequal global distribution
- more common in North America and Europe; rare in Asia

AETIOLOGY
Age:

Age (years)	Incidence
40	1 in 10,000
40–59	1 in 103
60–79	1 in 8

Risk at 50 years:
- 40% lifetime risk for latent cancer
- 9.5% risk for clinically apparent cancer
- 2.9% risk of death from cancer

Race:
- increased in Africans

Family history:
- 5–10% of cancers are inherited in autosomal dominant manner

Age of onset for 1 or more relatives:

Age of onset (years)	Increase in relative risk
70	4-fold
60	5-fold
50	7-fold

High dietary fat: ● relative risk increased by 2

Risk Factor	Relative risk
Obesity	1.25
Dairy products	1.30
Animal fat	1.31
Number of sexual partners	1.21
Vasectomy	1.54
Family history	1.70

GENETICS OF PROSTATE CANCER

● gene responsible for familial cancer located on chromosome 1
● regions identified so far: 8p, 10q, 13q, 16q, 17p, 18q
● increased plasma concentrations of insulin-like growth factor (IGF-1) associated with increased cancer risk
● decreased p27 (cell cycle inhibitor) reactivity associated with: higher Gleason grade, positive surgical margins, seminal vesicle

involvement and lymph node
metastases

PROPOSED GENETIC MODEL FOR PROSTATE CANCER

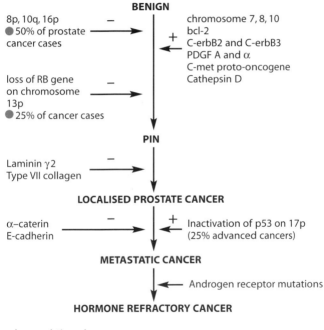

BENIGN

8p, 10q, 16p — →
● 50% of prostate
cancer cases

+ ←
chromosome 7, 8, 10
bcl-2
C-erbB2 and C-erbB3
PDGF A and α
C-met proto-oncogene
Cathepsin D

loss of RB gene — →
on chromosome
13p
● 25% of cancer cases

PIN

Laminin γ2 — →
Type VII collagen

LOCALISED PROSTATE CANCER

α–caterin — →
E-cadherin

+ ←
Inactivation of p53 on 17p
(25% advanced cancers)

METASTATIC CANCER

← Androgen receptor mutations

HORMONE REFRACTORY CANCER

- downregulation or loss
+ upregulation or gain

ANATOMY OF PROSTATE GLAND
3 zones to gland

Zone of gland	Volume of gland	Incidence of cancer in each zone	Comment
Peripheral	70%	60–70%	Most common site of prostatic intraepithelial neoplasia (PIN) and cancers
Central	25%	5–10%	-
Transitional	5%	5–10%	Most common site of benign prostatic hyperplasia (BPH)

HISTOLOGICAL MAKE-UP OF PROSTATE GLAND
3 principal cell types in prostate epithelium:

- secretory luminal cells – lowest proliferative activity
- basal cells – highest proliferative activity of prostate epithelium
- neuroendocrine cells – least common cell type

Pathology:

- 95% adenocarcinomas
- 85% cases multifocal
- other 5% • 90% transitional cell carcinomas
  • 10% neuroendocrine/ sarcomas

Cytology of Prostate Cancer
- hyperchromatic, enlarged nuclei with prominent nucleoli
- abundant cytoplasm
- ABSENT basal cell layer

PIN – precursor to prostate cancer

Cytogenetics of PIN
- PIN has cytological characteristics of prostate cancer
- difference is that basal cell layer is PRESENT in PIN

High grade PIN
- 80% associated with invasive prostate cancer
- when found on needle biopsy, 30–50% chance of finding carcinoma on subsequent biopsy
- therefore, these patients should have repeat biopsy to exclude missed invasive cancer

DIAGNOSIS OF PROSTATE CANCER

Digital rectal examination (DRE)
- subjective examination
- 21–53% positive predictive value
- only 30–40% of cancers diagnosed by DRE will have disease confined to the prostate
- underdiagnosis and overdiagnosis in 60% of patients if used in isolation

PSA

- produced by epithelial cells and secreted into lumen
- half-life 2.2–3.2 days
- false elevations occur after urethral instrumentation, prostate biopsy, urinary retention and prostatitis
- prostate-specific but not disease-specific
- BPH causes an average rise of PSA of 0.75ng/ml per annum
- exists in 3 forms:
  - free PSA (10–40% of total PSA)
  - bound to alpha-antichymotrypsin (ACT) (60–90% of total PSA)
  - bound to alpha 2-macroglobulin (this is not immunoreactive)

Free PSA:

- useful for patients with PSA 4–10ng/ml who may need a repeat biopsy
- ratio of 14–28% proposed as cut-off
- free/total PSA ratio:
  - <15% suggestive of cancer
  - >25% suggestive of BPH
  - 15–25 - unknown

PSA density:

- divide PSA by prostate volume
- PSAD >0.15 proposed as threshold for performing biopsies (rarely used)

PSA velocity:

- change in PSA/change in time

● rise of >0.75ng/ml in a year is cause for concern

Transrectal ultrasound (TRUS):
● sensitivity varies from 52–91%
● specificity for cancer 41–97%
● 80% overlap between lesions that are benign and those that are malignant
● majority of lesions are hypoechoic
● can detect extracapsular spread in >60% of cases

TRUS and biopsy:
● needle core biopsy underestimates tumour grade in 33–45% of cases
● overestimates in 4–32% of cases

Complications:
● haematuria (20–25% of patients for 2 days)
● infection (1–6%)
● haemospermia (9%)
● haemoatochezia (blood in stool – 9%)

Chance of cancer in biopsy

	PSA <4ng/ml	PSA 4 –10ng/ml	PSA >10ng/ml
DRE normal	6–9%	20–23%	Approx 50%
DRE abnormal	12–15%	53–56%	-

CT Scan:
● involved nodes >1cm diameter
● accuracy in identifying metastatic involvement of nodes is 40–50%

MRI Scan:
- overall accuracy of 69% for staging prostate cancer (local and advanced)
- better than CT for detecting local extension, but no advantage for lymph node metastases

Bone Scan:
- 24% of prostate cancer patients have bone metastases
- 1% false-negative rates

Indications:
- bone pain with any PSA value (43% with positive bone scan are asymptomatic)
- elevated alkaline phosphatase
- PSA >10ng/ml prior to intervention
- PSA >2.0ng/ml after prostatectomy

GRADING OF PROSTATE CANCER
Gleason Staging:
- based on degree of glandular differentiation
- reflects tumour heterogeneity
- >50% cancers contain > 2 patterns
- strong predictor of biologic behaviour of prostate cancer
- relies upon low power appearance of glandular architecture from 1–5
- obtained by adding the primary and secondary grades

Primary grade:
- most commonly observed pattern of cancer

Secondary grade:
- second most commonly observed pattern

Gleason sum or score (2–10)

2–4	● well differentiated
5–6	● moderately differentiated
7	● controversial – some believe moderately, others poorly differentiated
8–10	● poorly differentiated

TNM CLASSIFICATION (1997)
T – Primary Tumour

TX	● tumour cannot be assessed
T0	● no evidence of primary tumour
Tis	● cancer in situ (PIN)
T1	● clinically inapparent tumour not palpable or visible by imaging
T1a	● ≤5% of tissue in resection for benign disease has cancer
T1b	● >5% of tissue in resection for benign disease has cancer, or poorly differentiated
T1c	● detected from needle biopsy due to elevated PSA (can involve 1 or both lobes)
T2	● tumour confined to prostate
T2a	● tumour palpable by DRE or visible on TRUS on 1 side only
T2b	● tumour palpable by DRE or visible on TRUS on both sides only
T3	● tumour extends through prostatic capsule

Staging

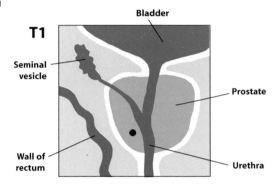

T1

Bladder

Seminal vesicle

Prostate

Wall of rectum

Urethra

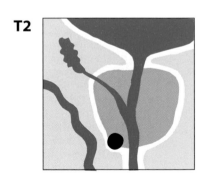

T2

T3

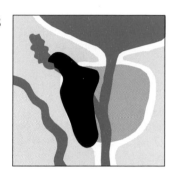

T4

T3a	● extracapsular extension (1 side or both sides)
T3b	● seminal vesicle involvement
T4	● tumour is fixed, or directly extends into bladder neck, external sphincter, rectum, levator muscles or into pelvic sidewall (does not include seminal vesicles)

N – Regional Nodes
(obturator, internal iliac, external iliac, presacral)

NX	● cannot be assessed
N0	● no regional lymph node metastases
N1	● metastases in a regional lymph node or nodes

M – Distant Metastases

MX	● cannot be assessed
M0	● no distant metastases
M1a	● distant metastases present in non-regional lymph nodes
M1b	● distant metastases to bone
M1c	● distant metastases to other sites

WHITMORE-JEWETT STAGING

A1	● ≤3 foci of carcinoma and ≤5% of tissue in resection for benign disease has cancer Gleason grade <7
A2	● >3 foci of carcinoma and >5% of

tissue in resection for benign disease has cancer Gleason grade ≥7

B1	● palpable nodule ≤1.5 cm, confined to prostate
B2	● palpable nodule >1.5 cm, confined to prostate
C1	● palpable extravascular extension
C2	● palpable seminal vesicle involvement
D0	● clinically localised disease with negative bone scan, but elevated serum acid phosphatase
D1	● pelvic lymph node metastases
D2	● bone metastases
D3	● hormone refractory carcinoma of the prostate

Risk of progression:
- grade
- age
- serum PSA levels
- clinical stage

PARTIN'S TABLES

(See Pages 64-67)

Partin's Table 1: Clinical Stage T1c (nonpalpable, PSA elevated)

PSA Range (ng/mL)	Pathologic Stage	Gleason Score 2-4	5-6	3 + 4 = 7	4 + 3 = 7	8-10
0-2.5	Organ confined	95 (89-99)	90 (88-93)	79 (74-85)	71 (62-79)	66 (54-76)
	Extraprostatic extension	5 (1-11)	9 (7-12)	17 (13-23)	25 (18-34)	28 (20-38)
	Seminal vesicle (+)	–	0 (0-1)	2 (1-5)	2 (1-5)	4 (1-10)
	Lymph node (+)	–	–	1 (0-2)	1 (0-4)	1 (0-4)
2.6-4.0	Organ confined	92 (82-98)	84 (81-86)	68 (62-74)	58 (48-67)	52 (41-63)
	Extraprostatic extension	8 (2-18)	15 (13-18)	27 (22-33)	37 (29-46)	40 (31-50)
	Seminal vesicle (+)	–	1 (0-1)	4 (2-7)	4 (1-7)	6 (3-12)
	Lymph node (+)	–	–	1 (0-2)	1 (0-3)	1 (0-4)
4.1-6.0	Organ confined	90 (78-98)	80 (78-83)	63 (58-68)	52 (43-60)	46 (36-56)
	Extraprostatic extension	10 (2-22)	19 (16-21)	32 (27-36)	42 (35-50)	45 (36-54)
	Seminal vesicle (+)	–	1 (0-1)	3 (2-5)	3 (1-6)	5 (3-9)
	Lymph node (+)	–	0 (0-1)	2 (1-3)	3 (1-5)	3 (1-6)
6.1-10.0	Organ confined	87 (73-97)	75 (72-77)	54 (49-59)	43 (35-51)	37 (28-46)
	Extraprostatic extension	13 (3-27)	23 (21-25)	36 (32-40)	47 (40-54)	48 (39-57)
	Seminal vesicle (+)	–	2 (2-3)	8 (6-11)	8 (4-12)	13 (8-19)
	Lymph node (+)	–	0 (0-1)	2 (1-3)	2 (1-4)	3 (1-5)
>10.0	Organ confined	80 (61-95)	62 (58-64)	37 (32-42)	27 (21-34)	22 (16-30)
	Extraprostatic extension	20 (5-39)	33 (30-36)	43 (38-48)	51 (44-59)	50 (42-59)
	Seminal vesicle (+)	–	4 (3-5)	12 (9-17)	11 (6-17)	17 (10-25)
	Lymph node (+)	–	2 (1-3)	8 (5-11)	10 (5-17)	11 (5-18)

Key: PSA = prostate-specific antigen.

Partin's Table 2: Clinical Stage T2a (palpable <$\frac{1}{2}$ of one lobe)

PSA Range (ng/mL)	Pathologic Stage	Gleason Score				
		2-4	5-6	3 + 4 = 7	4 + 3 = 7	8-10
0-2.5	Organ confined	91 (79-98)	81 (77-85)	64 (56-71)	53 (43-63)	47 (35-59)
	Extraprostatic extension	9 (2-21)	17 (13-21)	29 (23-36)	40 (30-49)	42 (32-53)
	Seminal vesicle (+)	–	1 (0-2)	5 (1-9)	4 (1-9)	7 (2-16)
	Lymph node (+)	–	0 (0-1)	2 (0-5)	3 (0-8)	3 (0-9)
2.6-4.0	Organ confined	85 (69-96)	71 (66-75)	50 (43-57)	39 (30-48)	33 (24-44)
	Extraprostatic extension	15 (4-31)	27 (23-31)	41 (35-48)	52 (43-61)	53 (44-63)
	Seminal vesicle (+)	–	2 (1-3)	7 (3-12)	6 (2-12)	10 (4-18)
	Lymph node (+)	–	0 (0-1)	2 (0-4)	2 (0-6)	3 (0-8)
4.1-6.0	Organ confined	81 (63-95)	66 (62-70)	44 (39-50)	33 (25-41)	28 (20-37)
	Extraprostatic extension	19 (5-37)	32 (28-36)	46 (40-52)	56 (48-64)	58 (49-66)
	Seminal vesicle (+)	–	1 (1-2)	5 (3-8)	5 (2-8)	8 (4-13)
	Lymph node (+)	–	1 (0-2)	4 (2-7)	6 (3-11)	6 (2-12)
6.1-10.0	Organ confined	76 (56-94)	58 (54-61)	35 (30-40)	25 (19-32)	21 (15-28)
	Extraprostatic extension	24 (6-44)	37 (34-41)	49 (43-54)	58 (51-66)	57 (48-65)
	Seminal vesicle (+)	–	4 (3-5)	13 (9-18)	11 (6-17)	17 (11-26)
	Lymph node (+)	–	1 (0-2)	3 (2-6)	5 (2-8)	5 (2-10)
>10.0	Organ confined	65 (43-89)	42 (38-46)	20 (17-24)	14 (10-18)	11 (7-15)
	Extraprostatic extension	35 (11-57)	47 (43-52)	49 (43-55)	55 (46-64)	52 (41-62)
	Seminal vesicle (+)	–	6 (4-8)	16 (11-22)	13 (7-20)	19 (12-29)
	Lymph node (+)	–	4 (3-7)	14 (9-21)	18 (10-27)	17 (9-29)

Key: PSA = prostate-specific antigen.

Partin's Table 3: Clinical Stage T2b (palpable >½ of one lobe, not on both lobes

PSA Range (ng/mL)	Pathologic Stage	Gleason Score				
		2-4	5-6	3 + 4 = 7	4 + 3 = 7	8-10
0-2.5	Organ confined	88 (73-97)	75 (69-81)	54 (46-63)	43 (33-54)	37 (26-49)
	Extraprostatic extension	12 (3-27)	22 (17-28)	35 (28-43)	45 (35-56)	46 (35-58)
	Seminal vesicle (+)	–	2 (0-3)	6 (2-12)	5 (1-11)	9 (2-20)
	Lymph node (+)	–	1 (0-2)	4 (0-10)	6 (0-14)	6 (0-16)
2.6-4.0	Organ confined	80 (61-95)	63 (57-69)	41 (33-48)	30 (22-39)	25 (17-34)
	Extraprostatic extension	20 (5-39)	34 (28-40)	47 (40-55)	57 (47-67)	57 (46-68)
	Seminal vesicle (+)	–	2 (1-4)	9 (4-15)	7 (3-14)	12 (5-22)
	Lymph node (+)	–	1 (0-2)	3 (0-8)	4 (0-12)	5 (0-14)
4.1-6.0	Organ confined	75 (55-93)	57 (52-63)	35 (29-40)	25 (18-32)	21 (14-29)
	Extraprostatic extension	25 (7-45)	39 (33-44)	51 (44-57)	60 (50-68)	59 (49-69)
	Seminal vesicle (+)	–	2 (1-3)	7 (4-11)	5 (3-9)	9 (4-16)
	Lymph node (+)	–	2 (1-3)	7 (4-13)	10 (5-18)	10 (4-20)
6.1-10.0	Organ confined	69 (47-91)	49 (43-54)	26 (22-31)	19 (14-25)	15 (10-21)
	Extraprostatic extension	31 (9-53)	44 (39-49)	52 (46-58)	60 (52-68)	57 (48-67)
	Seminal vesicle (+)	–	5 (3-8)	16 (10-22)	13 (7-20)	19 (11-29)
	Lymph node (+)	–	2 (1-3)	6 (4-10)	8 (5-14)	8 (4-16)
>10.0	Organ confined	57 (35-86)	33 (28-38)	14 (11-17)	9 (6-13)	7 (4-10)
	Extraprostatic extension	43 (14-65)	52 (46-56)	47 (40-53)	50 (40-60)	46 (36-59)
	Seminal vesicle (+)	–	8 (5-11)	17 (12-24)	13 (8-21)	19 (12-29)
	Lymph node (+)	–	8 (5-12)	22 (15-30)	27 (16-39)	27 (14-40)

Key: PSA = prostate-specific antigen.

Partin's Table 4: Clinical Stage T2c (palpable on both lobes)

PSA Range (ng/mL)	Pathologic Stage	Gleason Score				
		2-4	5-6	3 + 4 = 7	4 + 3 = 7	8-10
0-2.5	Organ confined	86 (71-97)	73 (63-81)	51 (38-63)	39 (26-54)	34 (21-48)
	Extraprostatic extension	14 (3-29)	24 (17-33)	36 (26-48)	45 (32-59)	47 (33-61)
	Seminal vesicle (+)	–	1 (0-4)	5 (1-13)	5 (1-12)	8 (2-19)
	Lymph node (+)	–	1 (0-4)	6 (0-18)	9 (0-26)	10 (0-27)
2.6-4.0	Organ confined	78 (58-94)	61 (50-70)	38 (27-50)	27 (18-40)	23 (14-34)
	Extraprostatic extension	22 (6-42)	36 (27-45)	48 (37-59)	57 (44-70)	57 (44-70)
	Seminal vesicle (+)	–	2 (1-5)	8 (2-17)	6 (2-16)	10 (3-22)
	Lymph node (+)	–	1 (0-4)	5 (0-15)	7 (0-21)	8 (0-22)
4.1-6.0	Organ confined	73 (52-93)	55 (44-64)	31 (23-41)	21 (14-31)	18 (11-28)
	Extraprostatic extension	27 (7-48)	40 (32-50)	50 (40-60)	57 (43-68)	57 (43-70)
	Seminal vesicle (+)	–	2 (1-4)	6 (2-11)	4 (1-10)	7 (2-15)
	Lymph node (+)	–	3 (1-7)	12 (5-23)	16 (6-32)	16 (6-33)
6.1-10.0	Organ confined	67 (45-91)	46 (36-56)	24 (17-32)	16 (10-24)	13 (8-20)
	Extraprostatic extension	33 (9-55)	46 (37-55)	52 (42-61)	58 (46-69)	56 (43-69)
	Seminal vesicle (+)	–	5 (2-9)	13 (6-23)	11 (4-21)	16 (6-29)
	Lymph node (+)	–	3 (1-6)	10 (5-18)	13 (6-25)	13 (5-26)
>10.0	Organ confined	54 (32-85)	30 (21-38)	11 (7-17)	7 (4-12)	6 (3-10)
	Extraprostatic extension	46 (15-68)	51 (42-60)	42 (30-55)	43 (29-59)	41 (27-57)
	Seminal vesicle (+)	–	6 (2-12)	13 (6-24)	10 (3-20)	15 (5-28)
	Lymph node (+)	–	13 (6-22)	33 (18-49)	38 (20-58)	38 (20-59)

Key: PSA = prostate-specific antigen.

DEFINITION OF EXTRAPROSTATIC EXTENSION

3 criteria:
- cancer in adipose tissue
- cancer in perineural spaces of neurovascular bundles
- cancer in anterior muscle

Gleason score	Histological characteristic	10 year likelihood of local progression
<4	Well differentiated	25%
5–7	Moderately differentiated	50%
>7	Poorly differentiated	75%

Stage	Incidence of positive pelvic lymph nodes in patients with apparently localised cancer
T1b	23–28%
T2a	7–24%
T2b	30–50%
T3	60%

Correlation of Gleason Score with Radical Prostatectomy Pathology

	Gleason score			
	5	6	7	8–10
Established capsular penetration	16%	24%	62%	85%
Positive margins	20%	29%	48%	59%
Mean tumour volume	2.2	2.7	5.1	4.0
Seminal vesicle invasion	1%	4%	17%	48%
Lymph node metastases	1%	2%	12%	24%

Localised Prostate Cancer (treated conservatively)

Histological grade	Risk of developing metastases	
	5 years	10 years
Well differentiated	19%	40%
Moderately differentiated	42%	70%
Poorly differentiated	74%	85%

Ten-year relative survival in early prostate cancer (compared with age-matched cohort)

Gleason Grade	Radical prostatectomy	DXT	Surveillance
2-4	1.17	1.17	1.01
5-7	1.11	0.93	0.78
8-10	0.87	0.63	0.36

Clinically localised prostate cancer	Radical prostatectomy	DXT	Surveillance and deferred treatment
Disease-specific 10-year survival	88.5-93%	66–74%	80–85%

Clinically localised prostate cancer	Number of patients		10-year metastases-free survival rate		10-year disease-specific survival rate	
	DT	RP	DT	RP	DT	RP
Well differentiated	492	541	85%	87%	87%	94%
Moderately differentiated	265	1743	63%	68%	87%	80%
Poorly differentiated	631	234	47%	52%	34%	77%

DT – deferred treatment
RP – radical prostatectomy

EARLY PROSTATE CANCER MANAGEMENT
1. Watchful waiting:
- involves careful observation and PSA monitoring at regular intervals
- treatment initiated when cancer causes symptoms or PSA values start to rise

Indications:
- patients older than 70 years
- low-stage, clinically localised prostate cancers (stage T1a)
- life expectancies <10 years

Rationale:
- 10–25% of these cancers progress within 10 years
- rarely advance significantly within 5 years
- 232 patients with T0-T2NXM0 were watched for a mean of 15 years when the disease-free survival was 81%

2. Radical prostatectomy:
- aim is cure
- 70% disease-free survival at 7–10 years

Indications:
- localised cancer
- life expectancy >15 years

Complications:
- <1% perioperative mortality (1–4%, depending on age)
- 30–100% erectile dysfunction
- 2–18% incontinence
- 27.5% mild stress incontinence
- 14 41% positive surgical margins

3. Radiotherapy (DXT):
- alternative to surgery
- useful for patients with T1 or T2a disease
- 53% survival rate at 15 years

Predictors of treatment failure:
- nadir PSA (cure defined as achievement and maintenance of PSA nadir < 0.5ng/ml)
- T stage

2 types:
a. Conformal external beam radiation

Complications:
- risk of second solid malignancy:
  - 1 in 290
  - 1 in 125 if survive 5 years after diagnosis
  - 1 in 70 if >10 year survival
- 48–59% erectile dysfunction rate
- patients who have had previous TURP or pelvic surgery are at greater risk of developing severe complications
- cystitis (8%), urethral stricture (4%), enteritis (3%), proctitis (2%)

b. Interstitial radiation

Complications:
- urinary voiding symptoms (12%), erectile dysfunction (10%), rectal discomfort (3%), oedema (3%)

GUIDELINES FOR PATIENT SELECTION

Surgical candidates	Radiation candidates
Life expectancy >10 years Age <70 years	Older men (late 60s-70s) Men who refuse therapy
Good general health	Multiple medical problems Poor surgical risk patients
Stage T1b, T1c, T2a, early T2b	All stages, including advanced stage T1b, T1c, T2, T3, T4
Well-differentiated tumours Moderately well-differentiated tumours	Well, moderately well and poorly differentiated tumours
Sexual potency important	Sexual potency less important

MANAGEMENT OF ADVANCED PROSTATE CANCER

- by definition, these cancers are incurable
- well differentiated tumours have a 10-year survival rate of 50%
- moderately or poorly differentiated tumours have a 10-year survival rate of 20–30%
- poorly differentiated tumours have a 10-year adjusted survival rate of 27%

1. Surgery:

- 50% of T3 patients have lymph node metastases
- hormonal downstaging with androgen deprivation followed by radical prostatectomy results in overall organ confined disease of 28%
- overall positive margin rate is 43% (52% for surgery alone)

Conclusion:

- neoadjuvant therapy does not seem to alter the long-term recurrence rate in men with T3 disease

2. Radiotherapy:

- mainstay of treatment for T3 disease
- 15–30% 10-year survival rate
- 25–35% of patients with T2 disease have microscopic residual disease
- 40–55% with T3 disease will have microscopic disease post-DXT

Five-year actuarial rates comparing radiation with and without LHRH agonists

	DXT alone	DXT + LHRH agonist
Overall survival	63%	79%
Disease-free survival	48%	85%
Local control	77%	97%

3. Androgen deprivation therapy:

- 80% of patients with disseminated cancer will respond to hormonal manipulation
- medical and surgical castration (bilateral orchidectomy)

PROGNOSTIC FACTORS FOR HORMONE RESPONSIVENESS

Factor at time of diagnosis	Outcome
Extent of bone lesions <6 metastatic lesions	Better 2-year survival
Alkaline phosphatase	Correlation with survival for stage
Haemoglobin	
Performance status	
Low serum testosterone	Poor response to hormonal treatment
Lower pretreatment PSA levels	Increased survival
PSA decline at 6 months <4ng/ml or 95% of baseline 4-49ng/ml or 90-95% baseline >49ng/ml or < 90% baseline	Progression-free survival 31–36 months 12–16 months 6 months

a. LHRH therapy:
- causes initial stimulation of FSH and LH and therefore an increase in serum testosterone
- after 3–4 weeks, they inhibit LH and FSH and decrease testosterone levels
- need to give antiandrogen at time of initiation of therapy with LHRH agonist
- up to 90% of patients with untreated metastatic disease respond to treatment with LHRH agonists
- studies have shown persistent suppression of androgen levels for 2 years

b. Maximum androgen blockade (MAB):
- rationale is that 20–25% of patients who relapse after orchidectomy are found to have high levels of serum DHT
- involves use of orchidectomy or LHRH agonist with an antiandrogen to block peripheral androgen action

	Progression-free survival	Overall survival
LHRH agonist alone	28.3 months	13.9 months
LHRH agonist and flutamide	35.6 months	16.5 months

Conclusions:
- combined therapy offers improved overall survival, but the survival

benefit must be weighed against the additional cost and inconvenience
- no compelling evidence that this method of castration offers any advantage over the other medical/surgical methods

c. Monotherapy with antiandrogens:

2 types of antiandrogens:
- steroidal with intrinsic hormonal activity • cyproterone acetate
- nonsteroidal that bind directly onto androgen receptor, but with no intrinsic hormonal activity
  • flutamide, casodex

Effectiveness of monotherapy

	Response rate	Mean duration of response
Cyproterone acetate	70–80%	18 months
Flutamide	50–87%	-
Casodex	57%	34 months

- 5-alpha-reductase therapy under investigation
  • finasteride

Early versus delayed androgen deprivation therapy?

- early therapy offers a survival advantage over delayed treatment, especially when the tumour burden is minimal

- early treatment also delays complications of late prostate cancer
- side-effects and inconvenience need to be discussed with patient and treatment individualised

TIME FOR CASTRATION METHODS TO TAKE ACTION

	Serum testosterone levels (ng/ml)	Time to nadir testosterone level
Normal levels	6.11+/- 1.82 (2.12+/- 0.63 µmol/l)	-
Surgical castration	0.2	8.6 +/- 3.2 hours
Diethylstilboestrol		
-1mg/day	0.8	7 days
	0.75	1 month
-3mg/day	0.2-0.5	38.3 +/- 15.5 days
LHRH agonist	0.2-0.5	+/- 3 weeks
MAB	0.2-0.5	+/- 2 weeks

d. Intermittent Androgen Suppression (IAS):

- involves initiation of antiandrogen therapy and then halting therapy upon a predefined clinical response (usually based on PSA level)
- aims to delay progression to androgen-independent state
- however, IAS does not prevent androgen-independent state

Typical regime:
- MAB for 6 months until PSA nadir reached
- median survival worse if PSA level >4ng/ml at this point
- consider IAS if PSA level stable at <4ng/ml
- withdraw therapy until PSA reaches pre-treatment levels and then restart

Results:
- patients are off therapy for mean of 41% and 45% over first 2 cycles
- mean time to progression is 128 weeks
- mean overall survival 52 months

HORMONE REFRACTORY CANCER
- majority of patients die within 12 months
- major dilemma

Options:
- withdraw antiandrogen therapy
  - 21% have serum PSA response
  - mean duration of response is 5 months
- corticosteroids
  - 50% decreases in PSA levels have been seen in 20% of patients
- antioestrogen therapy
  - poor response to tamoxifen (0-10%)
  - 43% overall response to diethylstilboestrol

- chemotherapy
  - no single agent or combination therapy has shown improved survival
- future directions
  - angiogenesis inhibitors, growth factor inhibitors, immunotherapy

COMPLICATIONS OF LATE PROSTATE CANCER

Bone pain:
- crucial to control for maintaining quality of life
- irradiation can provide relief in 75% of patients for up to 6 months
- bisphosphonates may help by inhibiting the activity of osteoclasts

Spinal cord compression:
- mostly in thoracic and lumbar regions of spine

Bladder obstruction:
- in 2/3 of patients on androgen deprivation therapy
- treat with indwelling catheter or ICSC for up to 3 months
- may need TURP

Anaemia:
- multifactorial
- may benefit from iron and vitamin supplements or erythropoietin
- blood transfusion may actually improve overall strength and performance status

ANALGESIA FOR ADVANCED PROSTATE CANCER

Oral morphine (mg)		Parenteral diamorphine (mg)	
Morphine sulphate (4-hourly)	Morphine sulphate – MR (12-hourly)	Diamorphine hydrochloride (i/m injection 4-hourly)	Diamorphine hydrochloride (s/c infusion every 24-hours)
5	20	2.5	15
10	30	5	20
15	50	5	30
20	60	7.5	45
30	90	10	60
40	120	15	90
60	180	20	120
80	240	30	180
100	300	40	240
130	400	50	300
160	500	60	360
200	600	70	400

Testicular Cancer

Incidence:
- 1–2% of all male cancers
- most common cancer in 15–35 year olds
- 2–3 cases per year per 100,000 men (UK) – varies in different countries
- lifetime risk 1 : 500 (0.2%)
- peak incidence 4th decade for seminomas
- peak incidence 3rd decade for teratomas

Aetiology:
- cryptorchidism
  - accounts for 10% of all cancer cases
  - increases risk 48-fold
  - 5–10% will develop cancer in contralateral normally descended testis
- familial
  - 1st degree relatives have 6–10-fold increased risk
- endocrine factors
  - increased FSH levels are predictive of increased risk

GENETICS OF TESTICULAR CANCER
- 2% of patients with testicular tumours have an affected family member, implying a genetic component

1. Gain of 12p most reliable • 80% of invasive tumours have
   an extra copy of 12p
    • not found in CIS
2. c-KIT (stem cell factor receptor) proto-oncogene expression
   noted in seminomas, but not in NSGCT
3. Yolk sac tumours show recurrent loss of part of 6Q
4. Spermatocytic seminomas are associated with gain of
   chromosome 9

HISTOLOGICAL CLASSIFICATION

● 90–95% are of germ cell origin
   • these cells are the most
     mitotically active
   • hence, more prone to
     developing DNA mutations
● <4% from supporting cells
   • these have low proliferative rates

REVISED WHO CLASSIFICATION OF GERM CELL TUMOURS (GCT)

A. Precursor lesion

B. Tumours of one histological type

    1. Seminoma

    2. Spermatocytic seminoma

Non-seminomatous germ cell tumours (NSGCT)

    3. Embryonal cancer

    4. Yolk sac tumour (endodermal sinus tumour)

    5. Polyembryoma

    6. Trophoblastic tumours
       Choriocarcinoma • a. Pure
                  • b. Mixed
                  • c. Placental site
                     implantation tumour

7. Teratoma
- • a. Mature teratoma
- • b. Immature teratoma
- • c. Teratoma with malignant areas

C. Tumour of more than one histological type
Teratocarcinoma
Choriocarcinoma and any other type
Other combinations

WHO CLASSIFICATION OF NON-GERM CELL TUMOURS (NGCT)
Sex cord and stromal lesions
1. Leydig cell tumours
2. Sertoli cell tumours
Large-cell calcifying Sertoli cell tumour
3. Granulosa cell tumours
- • a. Adult
- • b. Juvenile
4. Theca cell tumour
5. Undifferentiated
6. Mixed
Tumours and tumour-like lesions containing both germ cell and sex cord stromal cells
1. Gonadoblastoma
2. Mixed germ cell gonadal stromal tumours
Miscellaneous tumours
1. Gonadal hamartomas
2. Carcinoid
3. Others
Lymphoid and haematopoietic tumours
Secondary tumours

BRITISH TESTICULAR TUMOUR PANEL - OTHER CLASSIFICATION ASIDE FROM WHO

Seminoma
Teratoma differentiated (TD)
Malignant teratoma intermediate (MTI)
Malignant teratoma undifferentiated (MTU)
Malignant teratoma trophoblastic (MTT)
Yolk sac tumour

Presentation:

Seminoma	● 35–70%
Mixed tumours	● 60%
Embryonal cancers	● 3–6%
Teratoma	● 3% adults/38% childhood
Leydig cell tumours	● 1–3%
Sertoli cell	● <1%
Lymphomas	● 5% (50% in >60 year olds)

Metastatic tumours TO testis

	● mean age of 57 years
	● associated with poor prognosis
	● tend to occur after discovery of primary lesion
Primary sites include:	● prostate (35%)
	● lung(19%)
	● colon (9%)
	● kidney (7%)

Delay in diagnosis	● significant problem
	● delay by patient in seeking medical advice (ignorance, fear or embarrassment)

- delay by physician often due to maldiagnosis of epididymitis treated with antibiotics or secondary hydrocoele obscuring underlying mass
- delay not associated with advanced disease in seminomas

MEDIAN DELAY BY STAGE FOR TESTICULAR TUMOURS

Stage I	● 75 days
Stage II	● 101 days
Stage III	● 134 days

- delay with NSGCT associated with advanced disease and decreased survival
  - 8% mortality when diagnosis made within 6 months
  - 15% mortality rate with more delayed diagnosis
  - in disease-free patients, diagnosis made within 2 months, compared to 7 month delay in those who died of metastases

TUMOUR MARKERS

Tumour marker	Cell produced	Sensitivity for cancers	Half-life	Comment
Alpha-fetoprotein (AFP)	Yolk sac cells	• detectable in 93% of yolk sac tumours	5-7 days	Normal <10ng/ml
Beta-human chorionic gonadatrophin (hCG)	Placental syncytio-trophoblasts	• increased in NSGCT • 80% of embryonal cancers • all patients with chorio-carcinoma	24-36 hours	Normal <5mIU/mL
Lactate dehydrogenase (LDH)		• increased in seminoma and NSGCT • limited sensitivity		• correlates with bulk of disease
Placental alkaline phosphatase (PLAP)		• not very useful		• can be increased in 35% of patients without disease (especially if smokers)

● can be transiently elevated following onset of chemotherapy in 70% of patients in non-seminomas

● median time to peak 5 days (range 1–12 days)

Accurate predictor of treatment failure in patients with the following indices:

● >0.005 for AFP (ratio AFP from day 43/ day 1)
● >0.0025 for HCG (ratio HCG from day 22/ day 1)

STAGING
Imaging for testicular tumours

1. Scrotal ultrasound
● can detect intratesticular lesions 1–2 mm in diameter
● seminomas tend to be well defined hypoechoic lesions
● NSGCT are inhomogenous with calcification, cystic areas and indistinct margins

2. CT scan
● 44% false-negative rate
● less sensitivity for detection of micrometastases

3. CXR
● all patients should have a PA CXR

TNM CLASSIFICATION (1997)
T – Primary Tumour

● classified after radical orchidectomy, in which case suffix 'p' is added

TX	● tumour cannot be assessed (no radical orchidectomy)
T0	● no evidence of primary tumour (e.g. scar in testis)
Tis	● intratubular germ cell neoplasia (CIS)
T1	● limited to testis and epididymis; no vascular or lymphatic invasion; tumour may invade tunica albuginea, but not tunica vaginalis
T2	● tumour limited to testis and epididymis with vascular or lymphatic invasion, or tumour invades beyond tunica albuginea with involvement of tunica vaginalis
T3	● tumour invades spermatic cord with or without vascular/lymphatic invasion
T4	● tumour invades scrotum with or without vascular/lymphatic invasion

N – Regional Lymph Nodes

	● consist of abdominal para-aortic, preaortic, interaortocaval, precaval, paracaval, retrocaval and retroaortic nodes
	● nodes along spermatic vein are considered regionally
	● intrapelvic and inguinal nodes are considered regional after scrotal or inguinal surgery
NX	● cannot be assessed

N0	● no regional lymph node metastases
N1	● single ipsilateral lymph nodes ≤2cm in greatest dimension
N2	● multiple lymph nodes, or single lymph node >2cm, but <5cm in greatest dimension
N3	● nodal mass >5cm

M – Distant Metastases

MX	● cannot be assessed
M0	● no distant metastases
M1	● distant metastases present

S – Serum Tumour Markers

Sx	● marker not available
S0	● markers within normal limits
S1	● LDH <1.5 x normal, **and** hCG <5000 mIU/ml, **and** AFP <1000 ng/ml
S2	● LDH 1.5–10 x normal, **or** hCG 5000–50,000 mIU/ml, **or** AFP 1000–10,000 ng/ml
S3	● LDH >10 x normal, **or** hCG >50,000 mIU/ml, **or** AFP >10,000 ng/ml

MEMORIAL SLOAN-KETTERING CANCER CENTRE (FOR NSGCT)

Stage A	● confined to testis
Stage B1	● retroperitoneal nodes <5cm in maximum diameter
Stage B2	● retroperitoneal nodes >5cm and <10 cm in maximum diameter

Stage B3	● retroperitoneal nodes >10 cm in maximum diameter or clinically palpable (bulky)
Stage C	● spread beyond lymph nodes and metastases

ROYAL MARSDEN HOSPITAL STAGING SYSTEM

Stage	Details
I	● tumour confined to testis
IM	● rising concentrations of serum markers with no other evidence of metastasis
II	● abdominal node metastasis
A	● ≤2cm in diameter
B	● 2–5cm in diameter
C	● >5cm in diameter
III	● supradiaphragmatic nodal metastasis
ABC	● node stage as defined in stage II
M	● mediastinal
N	● supraclavicular, cervical or axillary
O	● no abdominal node metastasis
IV	● extralymphatic metastasis
Lung	
L1	● ≤3 metastases
L2	● ≥3 metastases, all ≤2cm in diameter
L3	● ≥3 metastases, one or more of which are ≥2cm in diameter
H^+, Br^+, Bo^+	● liver, brain or bone metastases

SEMINOMA STAGING

Stage	Details
I	● no evidence of metastases
II	● metastases confined to nodes:
	• A: maximum diameter ≤2cm
	• B: maximum diameter >2–5cm
	• C: maximum diameter >5–10cm
	• D: maximum diameter >10cm
III	● supra- and infradiaphragmatic nodes
	• Abdominal status A, B, C or D
IV	● extralymphatic metastases

Other staging systems: ● Boden & Gibb Staging (1951) for Seminoma
● modification of Samuels' Staging System for Advanced Disease

PREDICTION OF METASTATIC POTENTIAL

NSGCT: ● 30–50% with clinical stage I disease have clinically undetectable metastases

Predictors of relapse or recurrence in clinical stage I:
● vascular or lymphatic invasion

Seminomas: ● risk factors for relapse in low-stage seminomas:
• tumour size – 36% of patients with tumours >6cm relapse
• invasion of rete testis
• elevated β-hCG

Predictors of recurrence:
● histological type
● invasion of rete testis

PROGNOSTIC CLASSIFICATION OF GERM CELL TUMOURS

- developed by International Germ Cell Cancer Collaboration Group
- based on retrospective analysis of 5202 patients with metastatic NSGCT and 660 patients with metastatic seminoma

NON-SEMINOMATOUS GERM CELL TUMOURS

Good prognosis:
- 56% of patients
- 5-year survival is 92%

Primary site – testis or retroperitoneal area, and no non-pulmonary visceral metastases, and low serum concentrations of α fetoprotein, human chorionic gonadotrophin, or lactate dehydrogenase

Intermediate prognosis:
- 28% of patients
- 5-year survival is 80%

Primary site – testis or retroperitoneal area, and no non-pulmonary visceral metastases, and intermediate concentrations of the tumour markers

Poor prognosis:
- 16% of patients
- 5-year survival is 48%

primary site –mediastinum, or non-pulmonary visceral metastases, or high concentrations of the tumour markers

Prognostic classification of NSGCT	LDH (x upper limit of normal)	hCG (IU/l)	AFP (ng/ml)
Good (all of the following)	<1.5	<5000	<1000
Intermediate (any of:)	>1.5 -<10	>5000-<50,000	>1000-<10,000
Poor (any of:)	>10	>50,000	>10,000

SEMINOMAS
Good prognosis:
- 90% of patients
- 5-year survival is 86%
- any primary and no non-pulmonary visceral metastases and any tumour markers

Intermediate prognosis:
- 10% of patients
- 5-year survival is 72%
- any primary and no non-pulmonary visceral metastases and any tumour markers

Poor prognosis:
- no patients are classed as having a poor prognosis

FERTILITY IN TESTICULAR CANCER
At presentation:
- 25% have defects in spermatogenesis at presentation
- 50–60% will reveal oligospermia

- only 9% have prior history of infertility

- testicular cancer patients have increased anti-sperm antibodies compared to normal population
- approx 50% of patients have temporary hypofertility post-orchidectomy
- 50% of patients after chemotherapy have normal sperm counts by 2 years; 25% remain azoospermic
- 35% of patients achieve paternity post-chemotherapy

METHODS OF RECOVERING FERTILITY
Fertility prophylaxis:
- cryopreservation of sperm or ICSI
- 40–60% of patients with testicular cancer will have adequate semen analysis for sperm banking prior to initiating therapy

Minimum requirements:
- sperm concentration >20 million/ml and 40% motile sperm

MANAGEMENT OF TESTICULAR CANCERS
1. Radical orchidectomy
- inguinal approach
- avoid scrotal violation

2. Adjuvant therapy
- surveillance
- radiotherapy (DXT)
- chemotherapy
- surgery: retroperitoneal lymph node dissection

Seminoma

1. Stage I seminoma
- orchidectomy alone will cure approximately 85% of stage I seminomas
- with the addition of DXT, the cure rate approaches 100%

Radiotherapy:
- standard therapy is post-orchidectomy low-dose DXT to para-aortic strip
- 5-year survival rate is 95%

Relapse rates at 5 years

Stage	Relapse rate at 5 years
I	1.8%
IIA	10%
IIB	18%
IIC	38%

Surveillance:
- difficult, as abdominal nodes difficult to palpate and markers are negative
- rationale for surveillance due to slight increased risk of complications with DXT, which includes risk of a second cancer
- surveillance will avoid specific anticancer treatment in 85% of patients
- subsequent treatment may be more intensive in those who relapse

2. Stage IIA/B
- 95% disease-free survival after DXT
- 5% require subsequent salvage chemotherapy
- overall stage-specific survival is 98%

3. Stage II – bulky disease
>10 cm:
- 50–75% disease-free survival with DXT alone
- 82–94% disease-free survival with chemotherapy alone

Conclusion:
- accepted treatment of choice is combination chemotherapy

5–10 cm :
- 50% cure with DXT alone
- 50% relapse
- of those who relapse, only 40% are salvaged by chemotherapy
- DXT gives overall cure rate of 70%
- prophylactic mediastinal DXT leads to increased late morbidity and mortality

Conclusion:
- treatment of choice is combination chemotherapy, with 80–90% disease-free survival rate

4. Stage III/IV
- 36% cure rate with DXT alone
- combination chemotherapy cure rates of up to 90%
- 4-year disease-free survival rate of 90%

NSGCT
1. Stage I disease
UK:
- standard treatment is chemotherapy for recurrence or prophylaxis

USA:
- standard treatment is RPLND

Surveillance:
- 27% relapse rate
- 80% of relapses occur <12 months after orchidectomy

RPLND

	Node-negative	Node-positive
Cure rate	90%	70%
Distant dissemination	10%	30%

2. Stage II disease
Primary chemotherapy:
- 98% 3-year survival rate for stage IIA
- 96% 3-year survival rate for stage IIB

RPLND :
- 8% relapse rate

Low-volume pathological stage II disease:
- <6 positive nodes, all <2cm in diameter
- surveillance for 5 years
- 100% salvage rates with chemotherapy

Higher-volume pathological stage II disease:
- >6 positive nodes; any node >2cm
- adjuvant chemotherapy
- relapse rate <2%

3. Advanced stage NSGCT (disseminated disease)
Good risk
(criteria as above):
- aim of therapy is higher cure rates and reduced treatment related toxicity
- combination chemotherapy produces 80–90% disease-free survival rates

Poor risk patients:
- aim is to improve number of patients with complete response and increase tolerability of side-effects of therapy
- overall survival rate is 48%
- no regime yet really improves survival

2 newer treatments for this group:
High-dose chemotherapy with autologous bone marrow transplant (ABMT)
- 50% disease-free at median follow-up of 31 months

High-dose chemotherapy with peripheral blood stem cell support (GM-CSF)
- 67% progression-free survival

Post-chemotherapy surgery
- 20% of patients require surgery once tumour markers have normalised
- usually 6 weeks after chemotherapy

Resulting histology:
- 40% – necrosis/fibrosis
- 40% – adult teratoma
- 20% – residual NSGCT

RELAPSED TESTICULAR CANCER
- 20–30% will never achieve complete response with primary therapy
- 10% will suffer relapse following complete remission
- ifosfamide-based regimes produce complete response in >40% of patients with recurrent or refractory disease

Factors predicting survival with conventional dose salvage therapy
- prior complete response to cisplatin-based chemotherapy
- testicular primary site

Factors predicting inferior long-term disease-free survival
- initial incomplete response to cisplatin-based chemotherapy
- primary mediastinal site of disease

EXTRAGONADAL TUMOURS
- 1–5% all GCT
- association between Kleinfelter's syndrome and mediastinal NSGCTs

Seminoma:
- 35% all extragonadal GCT
- 60% of patients present with metastases

- locally advanced tumour prevents adequate surgical resection; small tumours can be resected with postoperative DXT to produce cure
- patients with disseminated disease are treated with chemotherapy

NSGCTs:
- 80–85% have metastases at diagnosis
- AFP elevated in 80% of cases
- hCG elevated in 30–35% of cases
- 40–50% cure rates with cisplatin-based chemotherapy
- 50% die due to progressive resistant disease

INTRATUBULAR GERM CELL NEOPLASIA (ITGN)
- precursor of seminomas and nonseminomas
- progression to invasive disease can take up to 15 years
- 50% will develop invasive disease in <5 years

Synonymous terms:
- CIS – not generally used, as term implies cells are of epithelial origin
- TIN – testicular intratubular neoplasia

Pathology:
- tumour cells found on basal membrane in inner side of seminiferous tubules (normally spermatogonia reside here)

Cytology:
- large, irregular nucleus
- coarse chromatin
- abundant cytoplasm

Risk factors for ITGN:
- 5% risk of ITGN in contralateral testis in men with unilateral testicular tumour
- 2–8% risk of cryptorchidism
- 0.4–1% risk in infertile men
- 35–50% risk of ITGN in one or both testis in men with extragonadal GCT
- higher incidence of ITGN in intersex individuals with Y chromosome karyotype

Diagnosis:
- can be made reliably by testis biopsy (ITGN tends to be patchy)

Management:
1. Orchidectomy (for unilateral disease)
2. DXT (bilateral disease)
3. Chemotherapy – no consistent efficacy demonstrated

Penile Cancer

Incidence:
- rare cancer in Europe and USA
- 0.4–0.6% of all male cancers
- 1–2 new cases per 100,000 men
- 25–75% have phimosis at time of presentation (most men in USA are circumcised)

Mean age at presentation:
- 55 years

Geographical variation:
- Increased incidence (up to 20%) in Africa and South America

Aetiology:
- Presence of foreskin
  - rare among Jewish population (circumcision performed as a neonate)
  - increasing incidence in Muslim community who are circumcised pre-puberty
  - adult circumcision offers no protection to subsequent development of disease
- Poor personal hygiene with possible role for accumulation of smegma
- HPV 16, 18, 33 – increase in incidence of cervical cancer among sexual partners of men with penile cancer

PRECANCEROUS LESIONS
- progression in approx 10% of patients

Bowen's disease — CIS, typically of the penile shaft

Erthyroplasia de Queyrat — one-third of patients may have simultaneous invasive penile cancer
- usually involves glans

Leukoplakia — commonly occurs in diabetics

Balanitis xerotica obliterans

Histology of invasive penile cancer
95% — squamous cell carcinoma

5-16% — verrucous carcinoma
- well-demarcated lesion that is a variant of squamous cell carcinoma

Remainder: — sporadic cases of melanoma, basal cell carcinoma, Paget's disease, Kaposi's carcinoma

SITES OF CANCER
48% — glans
21% — prepuce
9% — glans and prepuce
6% — coronal sulcus
<2% — shaft
14–16% — other

Delayed presentation common with penile cancer
- 15–50% of patients may delay medical care for >1 year (embarrassment, guilt, fear, personal neglect, ignorance)

● 30–60% have enlarged nodes in groin at presentation – of these, 50% are due to metastases and 50% due to inflammation

STAGING
JACKSON STAGING (1966) – CLINICAL STAGING

I	● tumour confined to glans penis or prepuce, or both
II	● tumour involves penile shaft or corpora; negative nodes
III	● tumour confined to penis, with operable inguinal lymph node metastases
IV	● tumour extends beyond penile shaft with inoperable inguinal or distant lymph nodes, or distant metastasis

Problems with the Jackson system:

● characteristics of initial primary lesion not stated
● nature and extent of nodal metastases not specified

TNM CLASSIFICATION (1997)
T – Primary Tumour

TX	● tumour cannot be assessed
T0	● no evidence of primary tumour
Tis	● cancer *in situ*
Ta	● non-invasive verroucous carcinoma
T1	● tumour invades subepithelial connective tissue

T2	● tumour invades corpus spongiosum or cavernosum
T3	● tumour invades urethra or prostate
T4	● tumour invades other adjacent structures

N – Regional Lymph Nodes

NX	● cannot be assessed
N0	● no regional lymph node metastases
N1	● tumour invades single superficial inguinal lymph node
N2	● tumour invades multiple or bilateral superficial inguinal lymph nodes
N3	● tumour invades deep inguinal or pelvic lymph nodes, unilateral or bilateral

M – Distant Metastases

MX	● cannot be assessed
M0	● no distant metastases
M1	● distant metastases present

Minimal diagnostic criteria for TNM designation

Primary tumour (T)	Regional and juxtaregional lymph nodes (N)	Distant metastases (M)
Clinical examination	Clinical examination	Clinical examination
Biopsy of initial lesion and histological evidence of grade	CT scan	Chest radiograph, CT scan
	Superficial inguinal lymph node dissection	MRI scan, bone scan (optional)
	Aspiration cytology if available (optional)	Biochemical markers

Classification of tumours at time of diagnosis

Stage	Incidence at diagnosis
Stage I	58%
Stage II	13%
Stage III	25%
Stage IV	4%

Five-year survival by Jackson Stage

Stage	No. of patients	5-year survival
I	434	65%
II	212	42%
III	164	27%
IV	30	0

MANAGEMENT OF PENILE CANCER
Treating the primary lesion

1. Circumcision
- for prepucial lesions not located near the coronal sulcus
- lesion must be small and non-invasive
- need adequate surgical margins and close follow-up

High recurrence rate post- circumcision:
- 22–50%

2. Mohs' microsurgery
- involves removal of skin layer by layer under local anaesthetic
- each layer excised is colour-coded
- first introduced in 1942
- excised areas heal by secondary intention
- glans often misshapen or absent after treatment

Indication:
- small, distal penile lesions (< 2–3 cm)

Results of Mohs' micrographic surgery in expert hands

Size of tumour	Outcome
Tumour <1cm	100% cure rate
Tumour ≥3cm	50% cure rate

3. Laser therapy
- useful for Tis, Ta, T1 and some T2 lesions

a. Nd:YAG laser
- wavelength of 1060nm

- produces deep tissue penetration (3–6mm)
- coagulates vessels up to 5mm in diameter
- local recurrence rates:
  - 10% for stage T1
  - 30% for stage T2
  - 100% for stage T3

b. CO_2 laser with operating microscope

- wavelength of 10,600nm
- only penetrates outer 0.01mm of tissue
- only coagulates small vessels of <0.5mm
- advantage of penile tissue preservation
- used for small superficial lesions
  One study: • 50% positive margins
  • 15% recurrence rate

4. Partial Penectomy

- for lesions near coronal sulcus, involving glans penis and distal shaft
- need 2cm margin proximal to tumour
- 6% local recurrence rate reported
- 5-year survival rates of 70–80%
- poor cosmetic and functional results
- alternative is glans excision and reconstruction with skin graft

Percentage of patients able to achieve vaginal penetration

Size of retained corpora cavernosum	Ability to penetrate vagina
At least 6cm	90%
4.0–6.0cm	45%
2.0–4.0cm	25%

5. Total Penectomy and Perineal Urethrostomy

- for proximal lesions that do not allow 2cm tumour-free margin
- bulky lesions involving shaft or base of penis
- lesions where penile stump would be short
- no local recurrences

6. Radiotherapy (DXT)

- preceded by circumcision which:
  - exposes lesion
  - reduces DXT morbidity
  - allows follow-up

Indications:

- young individual with small (2–3cm) lesion on glans or coronal sulcus
- patients refusing other forms of treatment
- patients with inoperable tumour

Treatment Modality	No. of patients	Nodal status	Local control	Surgery for recurrence or persistent disease	5-year survival	10-year survival
External beam DXT	26	N- and N+ patients	62%	19%	62%	36%
Implant	50	N- and N+	78%	20%	63%	52%
Implant	109	N-	82%	-	82%	59%
		N+		-	36%	18%

TREATING INGUINAL LYMPH NODES
Spread of penile tumour follows anatomical pattern of lymphatics

- firstly to superficial inguinal lymph nodes (8–25 nodes)
- then to deep inguinal nodes (3–5 nodes)
- followed by drainage to pelvic nodes

Most inguinal metastases occur <2–3 years following initial therapy

- need 2–3 monthly follow-up during this time

Indicators of spread of disease

- grade of primary tumour
- depth of invasion (94% of patients with positive nodes had >5mm depth of invasion)

Grade	Incidence of nodal metastases
Well-differentiated	1/19
Moderately differentiated	5/19
Poorly differentiated	16/16

- pathological stage of primary tumour
- presence or absence of vascular invasion
- presence of >50% of poorly differentiated cells
- location of tumour – better prognosis with distal tumours
- size – >3cm have worse prognosis

Incidence of lymph node metastasis

No. of patients	T-stage		Grade		
	Ta, T1	T2 + T3+ T4	G1	G2	G3
			50% (G1+G2)		75%
40	11%	61%			
	0	50%	4%	79%	100%
35			30%	70%	60%
102	14%	52%	29%	46%	82%
117	10%	56%			
28	0	67%			
53	6%	40%			
66			19%	65%	85%
81	5%	14%	0	13%	44%

Five-year survival related to extent of nodal metastases

No. of positive nodes	5-year survival
1 node	85%
1-6 nodes	54%
>6 nodes	40%
Bilateral nodes	12%
Extranodal disease	4.5%

INGUINAL LYMPHADENECTOMY

- only 50% presenting with palpable lymphadenopathy actually have metastatic disease
- therefore, treat with 4–6 weeks of oral antibiotics
- if persistent lymphadenopathy after antibiotics, should consider treating disease
- 20–30% of patients with positive inguinal nodes will have positive pelvic nodes

Five-year survival based on the characteristics of inguinal lymphadenopathy

No. of patients	Palpable nodes (%)	Clinically-positive nodes		5-year survival rate	
		Histology negative (%)	Histology positive (%)	Negative nodes (%)*	Positive nodes (%)#
190	-	64	20	-	26
88	35	36	20	72.5	45
153	39	63	10	69	33
34	29	40	-	75	20
576	82	47	38	89	67
34	24	27	42	77	0
110	36	26	40	100	38
414	50	51	39	87	29

* inguinal nodes negative on histology and negative clinically
# inguinal nodes positive on histology after resection

Time of surgery – immediate or delayed?

Five-year survival rate in patients undergoing immediate and delayed therapeutic lymphadenectomy

No. of patients	5-year survival rates	
	Immediate surgery	Delayed surgery
55	32%	50%
12	-	67%
13	50%	40%
14	50%	75%
37	59%	61%
22	57%	13%
23	88%	38%
102	62%	8%

Role of complete lymphadenectomy in clinically-negative patients

- debate arises from the fact that ilioinguinal lymphadenectomy is associated with high morbidity
- wound infection, sloughing of skin flaps, phlebitis, pulmonary embolism, flap necrosis, disabling lymphoedema of scrotum and lower limbs
- 1 event in >50% of patients

Question of unilateral or bilateral lymphadenectomy when patient presents with unilateral nodes?

- penile lymphatics drain bilaterally
- contralateral metastases are found in >50% of patients who present in this manner
- thus, bilateral lymphadenectomy is recommended

Timing of lymphadenectomy

1. Immediately:

- in this setting, bilateral lymphadenectomy is recommended if carried out at the time of presentation
- contralateral dissection can be limited to area superficial to fascia lata

2. Delayed:

- if patient presents with palpable nodes unilaterally sometime after initial presentation, bilateral node dissection is not indicated

Role of pelvic lymphadenectomy in the patient with palpable inguinal nodes

- incidence of pelvic nodes when inguinal nodes are positive is 15–35%
- limited survival with finding of positive pelvic nodes
- consider surgery in young man who has good surgical risk
- otherwise, consider adjuvant chemotherapy

Survival data

Stage	5-year survival (%)	10-year survival (%)
I	93	84
II	62	65
III	34	31
IV	0	0

RADIOTHERAPY (DXT) FOR INGUINAL NODES
Five-year survival rates compared with surgery for histologically-proven nodal disease

Treatment for inguinal nodes	5-year survival
Lymphadenectomy	50-67%
DXT	25%

Role of pre-operative DXT

Treatment Group	Extranodal infiltration	Groin recurrence
Pre-operative DXT	8%	3%
No pre-operative DXT	33%	19%

Role of adjuvant DXT in patients with clinically impalpable nodes

- 25–29% subsequently developed inguinal metastases

Conclusions:

- DXT appears to have no role in patients with confirmed lymph node metastases
- prophylactic DXT does not alter the course of the disease

CHEMOTHERAPY

- role is uncertain, as insufficient evidence

Single agent:
Cisplatin
- 15–23% partial response rate

Bleomycin
- 45–50% partial response rate

Methotrexate
- 61% partial response rate

Combination therapy:
Vincristine, bleomycin, methotrexate (VBM)

- 82% 5-year survival rate when used as adjuvant therapy
- 37% 5-year survival rate when treated with surgery alone

Cisplatin and 5-Fluorouracil

- 23% partial response rate

Conclusions:

- current data suggests role in regression of lymphadenopathy
- no data from prospective randomised trials

Urethral Cancer

Incidence:	●	<1% of all urinary tract cancers
Male : Female ratio:	●	7 : 3
Age:	●	most common in 7th decade

Factor	Male	Female
Length of urethra	Approx 21 cm	Approx 4 cm
Aetiology	• History of venereal disease 37% • Urethral stricture 35% • Significant urethral trauma 7%	• Urethral carbuncle 2.4% • Condylomata accuminata 23%
Cellular location	Prostatic and membranous urethra • transitional cells Bulbous and Penile urethra • stratified columnar and squamous epithelium	Proximal 1/3 urethra • transitional cells Distal 2/3 urethra • stratified squamous epithelium
Anterior urethral cancers	• Glanular (meatus, fossa navicularis) and penile urethra • Drains to inguinal nodes • 50% have metastatic involvement	Meatal and/or distal 1/3 of urethra • Drains to inguinal nodes
Posterior urethral cancers	Bulbous, membranous and prostatic cancers • Drains to pelvic nodes	• Lesions not limited to the distal 1/3 of urethra • Drains to pelvic nodes
Incidence of cancers	• Bulbomembranous 60% • Penile 30% • Prostatic 10%	
Histology of cancers	• Squamous cell cancers 80% • Transitional cell cancers 15% • Adenocarcinoma/undifferentiated cancers 5%	• Squamous cell cancers 60% • Transitional cell cancers 20% • Adenocarcinomas 10% • Undifferentiated/sarcomas 8% • Melanomas 2%

TNM CLASSIFICATION (1997)
T – Primary Tumour

TX	primary tumour cannot be assessed
T0	no evidence of primary tumour
Ta	non-invasive papillary, polypoid or verrucous carcinoma
Tis	carcinoma *in situ*
T1	tumour invades subepithelial connective tissue
T2	tumour invades any of the following: corpus spongiosum, prostate, periurethral muscle
T3	tumour invades any of the following: corpus cavernosum, beyond the prostatic capsule, anterior vagina, bladder neck
T4	tumour invades other adjacent organs

N – Regional Lymph Nodes

NX	regional lymph nodes cannot be assessed
N0	no regional lymph node metastases
N1	metastasis in a single lymph node <2cm in greatest diameter
N2	metastasis in a single lymph node >2cm, or multiple lymph nodes

M – Distant Metastases

MX	metastases cannot be assessed

M0	● no evidence of distant spread of disease
M1	● evidence of distant spread of disease

MANAGEMENT

	Management of Male Urethral Cancer	Management of Female Urethral Cancer
ANTERIOR CANCER		
Ta/ Tis	1. Open segmental resection 2. TUR with fulguration	1. Open excision 2. Electroresection 3. Fulguration
Fossa navicularis	Amputation of glans penis	-
T1/ T2 lesions	1. Penile amputation 2cm proximal to tumour and perineal urethrostomy (50% 5-year survival) 2. Radiotherapy (role not well defined)	1. Brachytherapy 2. External beam radiation 3. Surgical resection of distal 1/3 urethra
T3 lesion	As with T1/ T2 lesions	1. Local excision and urinary diversion 2. Radiotherapy
POSTERIOR CANCER – high incidence of nodal metastases		
	Pre-operative DXT, radical cystoprostatectomy, *en bloc* penectomy, urinary diversion and bilateral pelvic lymph node dissection	1. Pre-operative DXT, anterior exenteration with urinary diversion and bilateral pelvic lymph node dissection 2. Tumours <2cm in greatest dimension can be treated with DXT or in combination with non-exenterative surgery
5-year survival	15–20%	10–20%

Urethral cancer with invasive bladder cancer (only men)

- 10% of patients after cystectomy for bladder cancer have/develop urethral cancer distal to the urogenital diaphragm
- 34% of patients develop urethral cancer after cystectomy if performed for recurrent superficial bladder cancer

INDICATIONS FOR URETHRECTOMY
At time of cystoprostatectomy

- visible urethral tumour
- positive swab cytology of urethra
- positive margins of membranous urethra on frozen section at time of operation
- multiple bladder tumours that extend into bladder neck or proximal prostatic urethra

Alternative to urethrectomy at time of cystoprostatectomy

- monitor urethral cytology
- delayed urethrectomy